The Tree That Would Not Die

BY ELLEN LEVINE

ILLUSTRATED BY TED RAND

SCHOLASTIC INC.

New York

Library of Congress Cataloging-in-Publication Data
Levine, Ellen.
The tree that would not die / by Ellen Levine; illustrated by Ted Rand.
p. cm.
ISBN 0-590-43724-0
1. Treaty Oak (Austin, Tex.) — Juvenile literature. 2. Austin (Tex.) — History
— Juvenile literature. [1. Treaty Oak (Austin, Tex.) 2. Trees.
3. Austin (Tex.) — History.] I. Rand, Ted, ill. II. Title.
F394.A965T744 1995
813′.54 — dc20   94-8394
CIP
AC
12 11 10 9 8 7 6 5 4 3 2 1   5 6 7 8 9/9 0/0
Printed in Singapore
First printing, September 1995
Production by Angela Biola
Designed by Claire B. Counihan
Title calligraphy by Jeanyee Wong
The text face is Garamond Antiqua
by Fine Composition, Inc.
Color separations were made by Bright Arts, Ltd., Singapore.
Printed and bound by Tien Wah Press, Singapore.
The paintings in this book were executed in watercolors.
Printed on recycled paper.

Acknowledgments

Both Ted and I are deeply indebted to John Giedraitis for his most generous help in the research for this book. I also owe many grateful thanks to Tom and Hazel Perry, Mary Lou Levers, Pene McCain, Marianne Gabel, and Ken Rogers; and to Eva Moore, whose special editorial rigor has nurtured the book's growth.

In memory
of Debbie Ginsburg
—E.L.

To my son Martin,
champion of the ancient forest
—T.R.

One morning hundreds of years ago,
an acorn fell and grew in the earth.
And that was me.

And I grew.

And as I grew, I saw farther and farther
across the land.

When I was eleven and giving shade,
I had a good friend, a buffalo calf,
who nibbled grass nearby.
When he'd rub against my trunk,
Blue Jay, higher up in my branches,
complained about the shaking.
"He's just using you to scratch an itch."
But I knew Calf was also saying hello.

When the buffalo ran,
their hoofs pounded the earth
and kicked up dust for miles around.
My branches swayed, my leaves trembled,
and my upper roots quivered.
Blue Jay coughed and flew off until things
quieted down.

And I grew.

Soon I was so big, the First People
chose me as a meeting place.
Comanche, Tejas, Lipan Apache, Tonkawa —
they fought many a war among themselves.
But when they sat by me, they laid their
weapons down.

First People gathered my acorns and leaves,
and made sweet teas from them.
"Come home safely from the hunt,"
said the young women
as the young men sipped my tea.

They told of past hunting trips. And they
sang of the buffalo who kept them warm
with thick skin blankets, moccasins for
their feet, and robes for their backs.

The children climbed my arms and swung
in pairs. They chewed my leaf stems
now and then, but they never hurt me.
Never did they cut me with knives.
They knew my bark was like a buffalo skin,
protecting me and keeping me healthy.

They walked softly on the earth around
my roots, for they knew I couldn't live
without them.

And I grew.

One morning, a loud clanging
echoed over the hills and woke me
earlier than usual —
soldiers with swords
that banged against their armor.
When their swords were still,
I could hear the music
of their Spanish words.

After a time, more Spaniards came
and built churches and settlements.
"Tejas" they named the land, the
First People's word for "friendly people."

And still I grew.

One steamy day, four First People sat under my canopy. They waited for a man named Stephen Austin. I myself cannot say if he came, for it was a hot afternoon, and I dozed off. I do know that ever since that day I have been called "Treaty Oak," for it is said the First People and Austin made peace beneath my tent.

I was made a boundary, I'm told.
West of me the First People lived.
To the east, Austin's people.

And I grew.

The American settlers came
and cleared the land.
They cut down many relatives
and friends of mine to build their homes
and light their fires.
I was the "Treaty Oak," and so I was spared.

The land began to change. Trails became
paths, became lanes, became roads.
Farmlands were cleared, and crops were
planted.

There was a woman who had nine
children. She was always washing clothes,
smoking meats, putting up fruits and
vegetables. Once a week she'd visit, sit in
my shade awhile, and smoke her pipe.

And the Tin Man stopped by whenever he
passed through. He traded pots and pans,
sharpened knives and scissors. As good as a
newspaper was he. Told what was
happening in every town.

And I grew.

I was very large when I got word
that Sam Houston and his soldiers
had defeated the Mexican Army.
They captured General Santa Anna
while Sam Houston lay wounded
under a relative of mine.

"Tejas" became a separate country.

Five men rode up one day and rested their
horses near me. They were looking for a
place to build Austin, the capital of this
new country they called Texas. The first
man pointed to the river flowing nearby.
The second stretched out in a field of
bluebonnets. "The surrounding hills are
like soldiers guarding the town," said the
third. "Perfect!" cried the fourth, and the
fifth agreed. So the government came here
to Austin.

Government offices were built, and rooms
were filled with important reports and
important letters and important orders.
Archives, they were called.

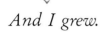

And I grew.

And the piles of reports and letters and orders grew. The people of Austin were proud of their archives. When the president of Texas tried to move the papers to another city, they shouted, "No!" They rolled a cannon into the street and fired it. No one was hit, but the president was forced to leave the papers behind. The people of Austin had won the Archives War.

I grew, but sometimes I didn't like what I saw. The First People and the settlers fought many battles. My boundary line was ignored. The settlers wanted to build new and bigger towns, and so they drove the First People from the land.

As I grew, Texas grew too,
and became part of the United States.
"The Lone Star State," we were called,
and the capital stayed right here in Austin.

Some settlers had brought slaves with
them. *People owning people — how can that
be?* I wondered.

Then slave-owners in Austin drove out
the Mexican-Americans. "Too friendly
with slaves," they said. "Makes the slaves
want freedom."

One moonlit night, a young black boy
and his Mexican-American friend
hid high up in me.
A group of white men searched for them.
I told Owl, perched on one of my arms,
to be silent.
The men rode past, and the boys escaped.

Still I grew,

tall enough to watch the cowboys
ride and rope amidst a sea of cattle flowing
toward Kansas.

Then the railroads came. Roads paved over
the grass, and more trees were cut.

I grew, but telephone poles grew too.
Houses pressed around me, and buildings
grew taller than I.
Everybody was very busy.

The owners on whose land I stood
talked of cutting me down to make room
for a building. For the first time
I was afraid.

Then something changed. People lost their
jobs and wandered past at all hours. I had
visitors who slept under me every night.
The Depression, or the Bad Times, they
called it. Once again there was talk of
selling me or cutting me down.

Still I grew,

but for how long, I wondered.

I think it was the children who saved me.
They sent pennies and nickels for the
city to buy me. And the city made a
park around me. There were picnics
and weddings, games and get-togethers,
all in my park.

I grew bigger, but the land around me
grew smaller. Buildings hid the sky.
At least I was safe.
I thought.

Then late one night a stranger
parked his car across the street.
He crept into the park and poured a liquid
in a circle by my side.
At first it felt cool, and I shuddered.
Later it burned.

I could not grow.
I could not grow!

My leaves turned brown and fell off.
The foresters and scientists were called in.
They cleaned the soil around my roots.
I was too sick to make food, so they tried
to feed me. I lost so many leaves, I burned
in the sun. They shielded me and
sprayed me with a cool mist of water.

I, who had shaded so many, could not
shade myself.

They cut my dead limbs away.
I am smaller now.

The man was caught and punished, but
he would not say why he had poisoned me.
Will I grow again?
I do not know.

I've had many visitors, sometimes a hundred a day. I didn't think so many people cared whether I lived or died. They sing to me, dance, pray, and leave presents. Many have brought me flowers. Some have read poems.

Thousands have written from around the world. "Dear Tree," the letters all begin. One boy wrote, "Please get well. You are too old to die."

Will I grow again? I do not know.

Wait!
I feel new buds pushing off the old leaves.
It's spring, and I am growing!
My new leaves are uncurling.
I hope they will last.

But if they don't,
my acorns are planted,
and they are my children.

About the Treaty Oak

For more than four hundred years, a mighty live oak tree, known as the "Treaty Oak," offered shade to the people of Austin, Texas. It stood more than three stories high with a crown of leaves that covered a quarter of an acre. Legend has it that Stephen Austin signed a peace treaty with leaders of native tribes under its spreading boughs. Although historians have found no evidence that the meeting actually took place, the legend persists.

Treaty Oak had survived floods, tornadoes, hailstorms, drought, bugs, and developers until March, 1989, when late at night, someone poured a powerful tree poison around one side of the tree. Months later, a passerby called the Austin City Forester to say the tree looked sick. That's when the poisoning was discovered.

Over $100,000 was donated to help save the tree. Scientists were brought from all over the country for the rescue efforts. They cleaned the roots and erected sunscreens. Thousands of people from around the world wrote to the tree, visited, and prayed for its survival. "Think of it," said John Giedraitis, the Austin City Forester. "All these people praying for a member of the vegetable family!"

A little over a year after the poisoning, a man was convicted of the crime and sentenced to nine years in prison and a $1,000 fine.

In the spring of 1991, almost two thirds of Treaty Oak had to be cut down. Four years later, however, standing with two braces, the remaining canopy still offers shade for those lucky enough to visit the tree.

Treaty Oak's acorns and cuttings have begun to put down their own roots. And through the efforts of a dedicated scientist, Treaty Oak has been cloned. That is, its very tissue has been cultured and transformed, so that identical copies of the tree can be planted. They will grow to shade the landscape across the southern states and California. One person tried to destroy Treaty Oak; others have helped to make it immortal.